# 5 SECONDS OF SUMMER

## SHOOT ☆
### FOR THE
# STARS

SCHOLASTIC INC.

Written by Mandy Archer and Steph Clarkson

© 2014 Scholastic. Published by Scholastic Inc.
SCHOLASTIC and associated logos are trademarks and/or registered trademarks of Scholastic Inc.
ISBN 978-0-545-81837-7
12 11 10 9 8 7 6 5 4 3 2 1      14 15 16 17 18 19/0
Printed in the U.S.A.  40
First printing, November 2014

# CONTENTS

# MEET AND GREET

INSIDE THIS BOOK YOU'LL FIND EVERYTHING YOU NEED TO KNOW ABOUT 5SOS, THE TALENTED GUYS FROM DOWN UNDER—

Luke Hemmings          Ashton Irwin

    Michael Clifford        AND
                         Calum Hood.

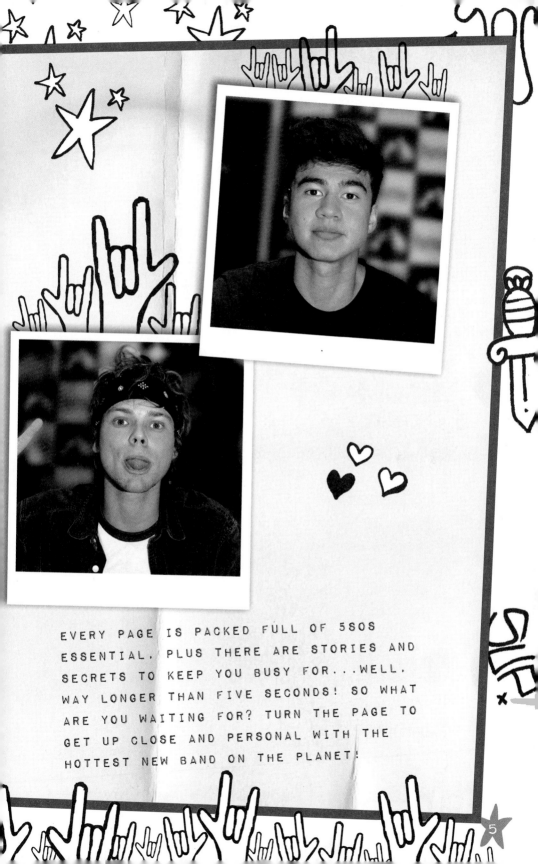

EVERY PAGE IS PACKED FULL OF 5SOS
ESSENTIAL. PLUS THERE ARE STORIES AND
SECRETS TO KEEP YOU BUSY FOR...WELL,
WAY LONGER THAN FIVE SECONDS! SO WHAT
ARE YOU WAITING FOR? TURN THE PAGE TO
GET UP CLOSE AND PERSONAL WITH THE
HOTTEST NEW BAND ON THE PLANET!

# SCHOOL DAYS

Back in 2011, Luke Hemmings, Michael Clifford, Calum Hood, and Ashton Irwin had no idea that they had the talent to make it in the music industry. The boys lived a quiet life in the suburbs of Sydney. Luke, Michael, and Calum grew up in Riverstone and were in the same year at Norwest Christian College. But they weren't exactly friends. Meanwhile, Ashton grew up about twenty-five miles away in a small town called Hornsby. He was at another school with a completely different set of friends.

Everything changed when the guys reached tenth grade. In February 2011, Luke, a gifted guitarist with a powerful voice, began to post clips of himself performing covers on YouTube. Word started to spread around the school and the local area. Before long Michael and Calum heard about Luke and went online to listen.

The three boys discovered that they all loved guitar rock from bands like Blink-182, Green Day, and All Time Low. Within weeks they had become friends. By April 2011, the boys had made the decision to form a band, and Michael eventually hit on the name 5 Seconds of Summer.

On April 13, Michael and Calum posted a clip named "5 Seconds of Summer Info!" onto YouTube and invited people to follow their new band pages on Facebook and Twitter. "We're basically only performing to our mums, they really enjoy us!" Calum joked. It was a humble start, but they'd made it official—5SOS was born!

In December 2011, 5 Seconds of Summer booked their first gig, but there was a problem—to play live they needed a drummer. Ashton, who had been playing drums for years, was lured by Michael's Facebook message inviting him to play "to 200 screaming fans." So Ash joined the trio and the boys soon posted their first cover.

# IT'S A DEAL!

5SOS continued to connect with their fans. They uploaded more videos so that there was lots of new material to enjoy on YouTube. It was through Facebook that the band hooked up with their first mentor and manager, Adam Wilkinson. Adam had unsuccessfully been trying to contact Luke, Michael, and Calum for months after meeting them in April 2011. In January 2012, he posted a message on the 5SOS page. Adam was the only male in a sea of female fans, so Ash immediately noticed and responded.

Under Adam's wing, the band performed along the east coast of Australia. Soon Matt Emsell of Wonder Management met the band and agreed to co-manage them.

Record companies and music publishers also came knocking. On Adam and Matt's advice however, 5SOS decided to remain label-less for the time being. This allowed them the space to grow, develop, and compose new material, while still holding on to their independence.

The group spent the next few months creating their *Unplugged* EP. It was released through iTunes in June 2012 and shot to number three in the charts! On the back of this incredible success, 5SOS landed an opening slot on a five-date Australian tour supporting Hot Chelle Rae.

THE 5SOS STORY

THE DIRECTION
CONNECTION!

It's crazy to think that 5SOS's biggest break was yet to come. In June 2012, Matt Emsell alerted Modest! Management, the team managing One Direction, to 5SOS's amazing online profile. By this time 5SOS had over 50,000 followers on their Facebook page and over 4 million followers on Twitter. By the autumn, Modest! had signed to manage the band.

On November 6, 2012, One Direction's Louis Tomlinson tweeted that he had "been a fan of this band for a while," posting a link to 5SOS performing "Gotta Get Out" from their *Unplugged* EP and adding a direct plea for Directioners to "get behind them." The Twittersphere went nuts! Directioners logged onto YouTube in the hundreds of thousands to check out the guys and show their support.

Despite all the attention, 5SOS focused entirely on their music. Soon they had enough material for their second EP, *Somewhere New*. The boys went on to release their first single "Out of My Limit" on November 19, 2012.

The video of the boys playing live received over 100,000 views within the first twenty-four hours. One of the viewers was One Direction's Niall Horan. He couldn't resist tweeting a link to the clip saying, "Just been shown this video. TUNNNEEEEE!" At this point 5 Seconds of Summer were still unsigned, but who needs a record label when you can count the world's biggest band as your fans?

In December 2012, the boys headed to London on a songwriting trip under Adam Wilkinson's watch. The boys had to do schoolwork in the morning, but then there would be meetings with record companies and time to hunker down to start writing.

# LONDON CALLING!

Ash explained how they were dealing with the pressures of mounting success. "We're very focused on what we need to get done and how hard we do need to work. We're very self-motivated," he said.

While in London, the boys from One Direction started spending time with 5SOS. "They're nearly the same age as us," says Ash. "I went and hung out at their rehearsal the other day. One day when we were in the studio, Niall came and hung out. We really got along with him. They're just normal people, to be honest. They're nice guys to hang out with."

The blossoming bromance led to another amazing announcement. Harry and company personally chose 5SOS to join their *Take Me Home* world tour as the opening act. The boys were overwhelmed. "I was like, 'Is this a joke?'" remembers Calum. The guys admitted to being worried at first about comparisons, but common sense told them to grab the opportunity with both hands. "People were already calling us 'the new One Direction' in Australia," said Luke.

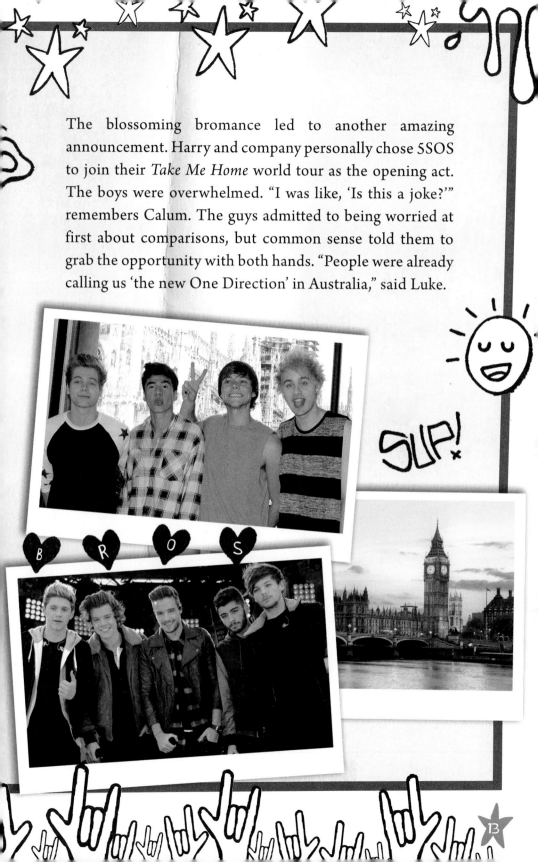

After the tour, it was time for Luke and the other boys to capitalize on the massive exposure they had received. Indeed, 5SOS's management decided that there was finally a deal on the table worthy of the group's talent.

## GOING GLOBAL

On November 21, 2013, 5SOS announced that they had signed to Capitol Records. The guys were super-excited and said, "Our team is awesome and really believes in us and our music. [They're] some of the best and coolest people we've met!"

On February 5, 2014, the band listed their worldwide debut single "She Looks So Perfect" for preorder on the iTunes Store. Within two days the track had reached the number-one

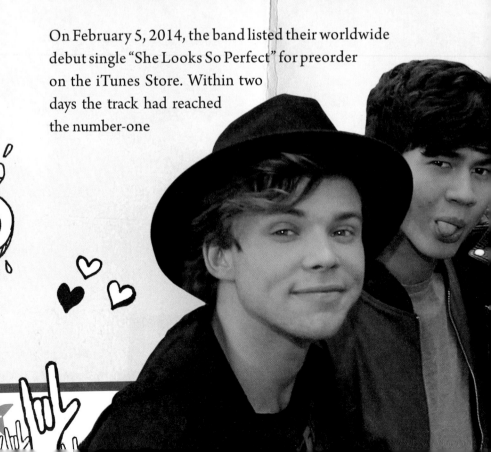

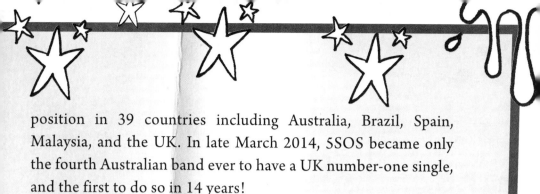

position in 39 countries including Australia, Brazil, Spain, Malaysia, and the UK. In late March 2014, 5SOS became only the fourth Australian band ever to have a UK number-one single, and the first to do so in 14 years!

A month later, Luke, Michael, Calum, and Ash revealed that they would again join One Direction on their 2014 *Where We Are* stadium tour stretching from May to October. On April 9, 2014, the *She Looks So Perfect* EP debuted at number two on the US Billboard 200 chart. Our four fave Sydney boys had finally gone global.

By the summer of 2014 the wait was finally over. On June 27, the boys released their debut studio album, *5 Seconds of Summer*, in Europe, Australia, and Asia. Recorded in LA and London, it is packed with rock guitar and big pop hooks. Unsurprisingly, the album rocketed straight to number one in Australia, Italy, New Zealand, Ireland, and the Netherlands. In the United States, the album shot straight to number one on the Billboard 200 chart and sold over 250,000 copies within the first week.

# AWARDS & ALBUMS

## TRACK LIST

1. "SHE LOOKS SO PERFECT"
2. "DON'T STOP"
3. "GOOD GIRLS"
4. "KISS ME KISS ME"
5. "18"
6. "EVERYTHING I DIDN'T SAY"
7. "BESIDE YOU"
8. "END UP HERE"
9. "LONG WAY HOME"
10. "HEARTBREAK GIRL"
11. "ENGLISH LOVE AFFAIR"
12. "AMNESIA"

The boys are unstoppable! Check out the list of awards and nominations that the group has racked up.

# 2014 WINNERS

RELENTLESS KERRANG!          Best International Newcomer
NICKELODEON KID'S CHOICE     Fave Hot New Band
TRL AWARDS                   Best International Newcomer

# 2013 WINNERS

MTV AWARD          Breakthrough Band
CHANNEL V          Australian Artist

Will they have a clean sweep in these forthcoming awards, too? Fingers crossed for 5SOS!

# 2014 NOMINATIONS

WE LOVE POP AWARDS:          Best Newcomer
                             Best Fandom
                             Best Summer Anthem
                             Fittest Boy on the Planet—all
                             Nicest Pop Star—Ashton
YOUNG HOLLYWOOD:             Breakout Music Artist
TEEN CHOICE AWARDS:          Choice Music: Group
MTV EUROPE:                  Best Push Act
MTV VMAS:                    Artist to Watch

FULL NAME: LUKE ROBERT HEMMINGS
DOB: JULY 16, 1996
ZODIAC SIGN: CANCER
FAVORITE MOVIE: ANCHORMAN
FAVORITE ALBUM: *TAKE OFF YOUR PANTS AND JACKET* BY BLINK-182
HOBBIES: SNOWBOARDING AND SOCCER
FAMILY: MOM AND DAD LISA AND ANDREW HEMMINGS, BROTHERS BEN AND JACK.
PETS: A DOG NAMED MOLLY
CELEB CRUSH: MILA KUNIS

Luke loves . . .
- Penguins. **He can't get enough of the cute creatures! Even his Instagram handle is @luke_is_a_penguin.**

- Ice cream. **Luke won the 5SOS Pizza Hut ice-cream eating competition, managing to munch through seventeen bowls of the stuff!**

Luke in a nutshell . . .
- Musical
- Cheerful
- Shy

LUKE HEMMINGS

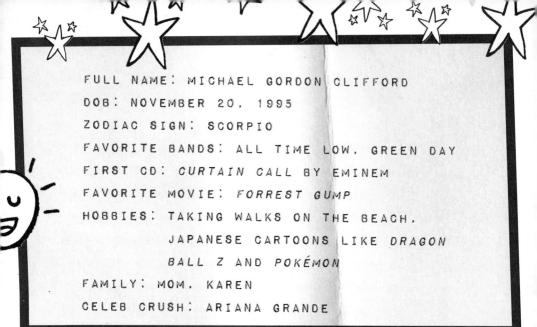

FULL NAME: MICHAEL GORDON CLIFFORD
DOB: NOVEMBER 20, 1995
ZODIAC SIGN: SCORPIO
FAVORITE BANDS: ALL TIME LOW, GREEN DAY
FIRST CD: *CURTAIN CALL* BY EMINEM
FAVORITE MOVIE: *FORREST GUMP*
HOBBIES: TAKING WALKS ON THE BEACH,
        JAPANESE CARTOONS LIKE *DRAGON*
        *BALL Z* AND *POKÉMON*
FAMILY: MOM, KAREN
CELEB CRUSH: ARIANA GRANDE

Michael loves . . .
• His computer. He says he can't live
  without it. Literally.

• His "reverse skunk" 'do. Naturally blond
  Michael loves changing his hair color.
  He once claimed that he'd rather eat
  an entire jar of Vegemite than shave
  his head.

Michael in a nutshell . . .
• Wild
• Hair-tastic
• Funny

MICHAEL
CLIFFORD

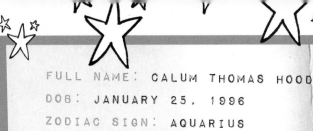

```
FULL NAME: CALUM THOMAS HOOD
DOB: JANUARY 25, 1996
ZODIAC SIGN: AQUARIUS
FAVORITE BAND: ALL TIME LOW
FIRST CD: I MISS YOU BY BLINK-182
HOBBIES: SOCCER — CALUM SUPPORTS LIVERPOOL FC
         AND ALSO LOVES PLAYING FIFA
FAMILY: MOM AND DAD JOY AND DAVID, SISTER,
        MALI-KOA.
PETS: CALUM LOVES DOGS, ESPECIALLY CUTE
      PUPPIES. HE DOESN'T OWN ONE, BUT IS
      OFTEN PHOTOGRAPHED WITH ASHTON'S POOCH,
      INDIE.
CELEB CRUSH: KATY PERRY
```

Calum likes . . .
- Pizza. **It's his favorite food.**

- Tattoos. **Calum has the Roman numerals "MMXII" inked on his right collarbone. This means "2012" and is said to be a tribute to the year that 5 Seconds of Summer was truly formed.**

Calum in a nutshell . . .
- Chill
- Adventurous
- Cuddly

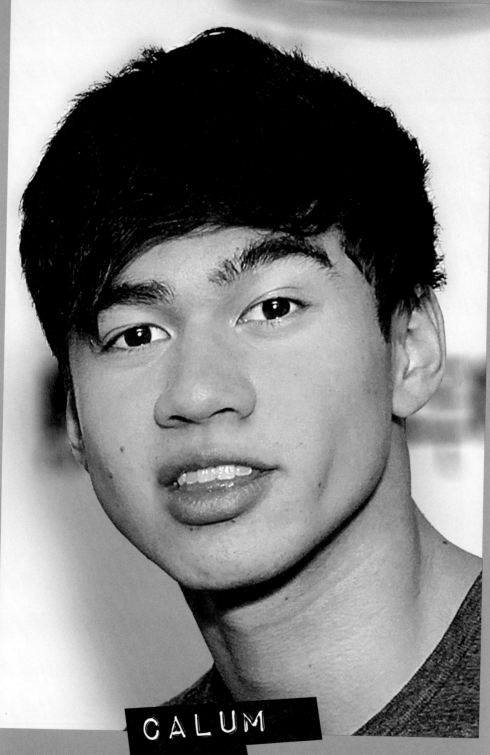

CALUM HOOD

FULL NAME: ASHTON FLETCHER IRWIN
DOB: JULY 7, 1994
ZODIAC SIGN: CANCER
FAVORITE BANDS: COLDPLAY AND JAMES MORRISON
FAVORITE ALBUM: *BULLET IN A BIBLE* BY GREEN DAY
FAVORITE MOVIE: *THE PURSUIT OF HAPPYNESS*
SIGNIFICANT OTHERS: MOM, ANNE MARIE; BROTHER,
                    HARRY; AND SISTER, LAUREN
PETS: A DOG, INDIE
CELEB CRUSH: HAYLEY WILLIAMS FROM PARAMORE OR
             JADE FROM LITTLE MIX

Ashton loves . . .
• Laughing. He's always cracking up,
  especially in interviews!

• Customizing old T-shirts into tank tops.

Ashton in a nutshell . . .
• Talkative
• Honorable
• Friendly

ASHTON
IRWIN

## 1

THE DEBUT CHART RANKING OF *SHE LOOKS SO PERFECT* IN AUSTRALIA AND THE UK.

## 2

THE SPOT THE SINGLE HIT IN THE US BILLBOARD CHART.

## 3

THE PLACE THE BOYS' EP EARNED IN THE US ITUNES CHART, BASED ON PREORDERS ALONE.

## 5

HOW MANY MINUTES IT TOOK FOR THE 5SOS UK AND US TOURS TO SELL OUT.

## 17

THE NUMBER OF BOWLS OF PIZZA HUT ICE CREAM THAT LUKE ONCE MANAGED TO EAT IN A SINGLE SITTING!

## 42

THE NUMBER OF COUNTRIES THAT *SHE LOOKS SO PERFECT* HAS TOPPED THE CHARTS IN.

## 100 +

THE NUMBER OF SONGS THAT 5SOS PENNED IN PREPARATION FOR THEIR FIRST ALBUM.

# 6,191

THE POPULATION OF RIVERSTONE, NEW SOUTH WALES—LUKE, MIKE, AND CALUM'S HOMETOWN.

# 80,000

THE ESTIMATED CROWD THAT THE GUYS PERFORMED TO AT THE CAPITAL FM SUMMERTIME BALL.

# 1,000,000

THE NUMBER OF VIEWS BAGGED BY THE *SHE LOOKS SO PERFECT* MUSIC VIDEO WITHIN THE FIRST 24 HOURS OF RELEASE.

# 1.7 million +

THE NUMBER OF HITS ON THE GUYS' ACOUSTIC COVER OF *NEXT TO YOU* BY CHRIS BROWN AND JUSTIN BIEBER.

# 2 million +

5SOS FOLLOWERS ON INSTAGRAM.

# 6.2 million +

5SOS FANS ON FACEBOOK

# 4 million +

@5SOS FOLLOWERS ON TWITTER.

# 12,700,000 +

COMBINED TWITTER FOLLOWERS.

10. Luke carries a hairbrush with him everywhere he goes.

9. The boys made up a new verb— "banding." The word can be used to refer to absolutely anything to do with the band.

8. Michael says he'd like to wear a superhero costume all the time as a fashion statement.

7. Ash loves vanilla-scented candles.

6. When the guys compose music, they usually write with other people and work in groups of two.

5. Luke has never seen the film *Titanic*. Gasp!

**4.** The boys each have their own favorite Teenage Mutant Hero Turtle.

**3.** 5SOS have their hair styled by Lou Teasdale. She is also the stylist for 1D.

**2.** Ash thinks that jet lag from traveling all the time helps him to be more creative.

**1.** Michael came up with the band's name during a math lesson.

# ONE LAST LOOK!

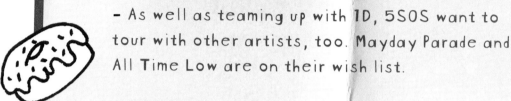

- As well as teaming up with 1D, 5SOS want to tour with other artists, too. Mayday Parade and All Time Low are on their wish list.

- Sometimes when they perform, fans throw My Little Pony toys at the band!

- 5SOS have guested at some mega events, too. Check out their live performances at the US Billboards awards and the Capital FM Summertime Ball.

- The boys once tweeted their fans, asking them to dress up as fruit. Hordes of girls turned up wearing kiwi and banana costumes!

- 5SOS have to watch out for some of the gifts that the fans throw at them. Once someone hurled a Rubik's Cube out of the crowd!

- The boys don't have particular backstage rules, but they do like the dressing room to be quiet and calm before going out to play.

- It takes a big team of professionals to put on a 5SOS gig. The guys call them their "tour family."

- Although 5SOS miss Australia from time to time, they never get too homesick. Their friendship keeps them going on the road. Calum put it best when he said, "Where the band is, home is."

# FAST FORWARD 5 SECONDS

Stand back—5SOS have BIG plans for the future! Luke, Michael, Calum, and Ash were out on the road with One Direction all through the summer of 2014. They wowed fans across the globe, from Barcelona to Chicago. After that, the band will be hitting arenas in 2015 with their own headline *Rock Out With Your Socks Out* Tour.

So there's definitely no sign that the boys will be putting the brakes on. Brace yourself for more sizzling new singles and music vids that are so hot you'll be playing them on permanent loop.

Expect the unexpected, too. 5 Seconds of Summer aren't like other boy bands. Their story might be sensational, but it's only just begun . . .